WILD WINES

by

Darcy Williamson

— A MAVERICK PUBLICATION —

Cover photo by
Dorian Copenhaver

Copyright © 1980 by Darcy Williamson

All rights reserved. No part of the material protected by this copyright notice may be reproduced or utilized in any form or by any means, electronic or mechanical, including photocopying, recording, or by any informational storage and retrieval system without written permission from the copyright owner. Printed in the United States of America.

Maverick Publications
Drawer 5007 • Bend, Oregon 97701

Dedicated to Dad

Table of Contents

Chapters

- I. Before You Begin 1
- II. Wild Berry Wine 9
- III. Wild Flower Wine 39
- IV. Wild Fruit Wine 57
- V. Wild Blends 69
- VI. Miscellaneous Wild Wine 85

Chapter 1

Before You Begin

The first time I picked up a book on wine making at home, I quickly became discouraged. As I scanned the pages, I noted such wine ingredients as Campden tablets, various types of wine yeasts, yeast nutrient tablets, malic acid, grape tannin, and pectic enzyme. As though this hadn't confused me enough, I scanned a little further and found such terms as hydrometer, must, racking, yeast starter, gravity, and bung. These ingredients and terms, which later became known to me, left me totally baffled at the time. I quickly decided that making wine was not a good project to begin on a quiet Sunday afternoon. I ended up using my freshly picked wild berries in pies.

Some time later I came across a recipe, published in an outdated copy of *Farmer's Almanac,* for Dandelion Wine. The recipe contained no foreign sounding ingredients and the instructions were easy to follow. For a novice winemaker, such a recipe proved inspirational. Winemaking, using wild fruits and flowers, later became one of my casual pastimes.

Since winemaking is not a full-fledged hobby, I have not become a connisseur of fine homemade wine nor an amateur scientist with a well equipped laboratory. My wines are flavorful and palatable even though they begin their existence in a cracked crock I purchased at a garage sale.

The methods I employ in wine making are very basic and unsophisticated. Most of the winemaking books currently on the market employ complicated procedures and expensive equipment. These books provide excellent information and technique for the avid home winemaker. However, most novice wine makers, as myself, prefer to begin with the basics:

Wild Fruit and Berries

Wild fruit and berries are free for the picking. This keeps the production cost of the wine at a very low level.

The fruit or berries should be fully ripened (unless otherwise specified in the recipe) but not over-ripe. A good thing to avoid is harvesting the fruit along roadsides or ditch banks which may have been sprayed for foliage control or insect pests.

Stems and leaves need to be discarded and the fruit rinsed and drained. Any bruises must be removed from the fruit. It is also a good idea to remove any little aphids, worms, ants, or other life crawling in and among the fruit or berries.

The flavor from fleshy fruits, such as apples, is best extracted if the fruit is run through a food mill before being placed in the crock.

Prepared fruit and berries may be placed in freezer bags and frozen until the time is convenient for using them. Frozen fruit or berries go directly from the freezer bag into the crock.

Wild Flowers

Wild Flowers should be gathered on a dry, warm day. Remove all stems, leaves, and green parts from the petals since any green will impart an off taste to the wine. Flower petals should be used within two days of gathering. If this is not feasible, the petals may be dried on racks in a warm oven, then stored in tightly covered containers until needed.

Other Wild Things

Wine can be made from numerous unusual substances. Grass clippings, maple leaves, barley, and hedge trimmings have all been used successfully.

I have included recipes for some unusual wine making ingredients found in the wilds. These include stinging nettles, sassafras bark, and birch sap. Instructions in gathering and preparing such ingredients for wine are included in the individual recipes.

Crock

I use the term crock throughout the following recipes. This doesn't mean you should rush out and buy one. A polythene trash can or pail will also work and is considerably cheaper.

If you are fortunate enough to have a crock handy, by all means use it. It is the preferred receptacle. However, if you are unfortunate in that you have a cracked crock, don't despair, they can often be fixed. One method for repairing leaks from small cracks is to fill the damaged crock with hot water, then rub the crack with a bar of paraffin. It may take a good deal of rubbing, but this method corrected the leak in my garage sale special. If the leak is too large to be remedied in this manner, try sealing the leak with rubber cement. Plaster has also been known to work. Don't attempt to repair the crock from the inside with any of these methods.

If your polythene trash can or pail leaks, get rid of it and spring for a new one.

Before fruit is placed in the crock or pail, it is essential for the receptacle to be clean. There are numerous methods of accomplishing this. The one I use is to wash the container with detergent, then make certain it is well rinsed. The container is then filled two-thirds full with boiling water and one half cup of baking soda is added. After ten to fifteen minutes the water-soda solution is poured out and the container rinsed with hot water.

Once the winemaking project begins, the opening of the crock should be covered. This prevents dust, flies, spiders, and other undesirable substances from falling into the concoction. Cheese cloth works well. Stretch a piece a couple of layers in thickness across the opening of the container. Secure cloth in place with string.

Some crocks and polythene pails come equipped with lids. In such cases, use the lids and forget the cheese cloth and string. But be certain that the lids are clean.

Water

Water is almost always added to fruit, berries, or flowers during wine making. Tap water is fine to use if it isn't ladened with impurities or chemicals. If you enjoy drinking your tap water, use it in making the wine. However, if you find your drinking water unpleasant, it would be advisable to use bottled water.

Extracting Juice

After allowing the fruit and water to stand in the crock the recommended number of hours or days, it is time to remove the liquid from the pulp. This is by far the messiest step of the entire project (unless one of the wine bottles later explode during storage).

I use the pillow case method for extracting juice. Sterilize an old, hole-free pillow case by submerging it in a pan of boiling water for five minutes. Allow it to cool, then use it to line a clean crock or container, folding the opening over the rim. Dump fruit and liquid into pillow case lined container. Tie a nylon cord or sturdy rope around the pillow case opening. Suspend the bundle from a cupboard handle or door knob so that it hangs just inside the container. Allow the juice to drip into the container. It wouldn't hurt to squeeze the pillow case once in awhile to speed things up a bit. When all the juice has been extracted, discard pulp and rinse out the pillow case.

Sugar

Experts say never add sugar directly to the extracted juice. I won't say "never," because I've done it that way and no one has known the difference. There is a better way to add sugar than by just dumping it in and stirring until it dissolves. Make a syrup. This takes a little more time, but in the long run, gives better results. Remove a few pints of extracted juice to a saucepan. Add sugar, then place pan over medium heat until sugar dissolves. Allow the syrup to cool, them stir it into the juice in crock or pail.

Yeast

If your extracted juice is bubbling, frothing, or acting in a similar strange manner, wild yeasts have infested the juice. Be joyful! You've just saved the price of a packet of yeast!

Yeast will need to be added if fermentation hasn't taken place naturally a few days after sugar was added. Both active dry yeast and compressed cake yeast will begin fermentation and both are available at most food stores.

In most instances, the yeast is sprinkled over the surface of the liquid in the crock. But some fruits and berries are more difficult to ferment and these require simple yeast starters. The ingredients and methods for preparing the starters are included in the recipes requiring them.

Once yeast has been added, the fermenting liquid shouldn't get any cooler than 60°F. or warmer than 75°F. A variance above or below these temperatures may inhibit or destroy the growth of the yeast.

Jugs

The fermenting future wine is usually transferred from the crock or pail to jugs. This is done to discourage bacteria from entering the fermentating juice. Cider jugs or used one gallon wine bottles make good fermentation jugs. Be certain that the containers have been sterilized by being submerged in boiling water for five minutes.

Juice is easily transferred from crock to jugs with the use of a sterilized Pyrex measuring cup. If such a measuring cup is not at hand, use a sterilized dipper funnel. A sterilized pitcher also works well.

Fill the jugs to about two inches from the opening. The mouth of the jugs must now be covered in such a way as to allow gas formed during the fermenting stage to escape, while preventing air and bacteria from entering. This is not as difficult as you may think. Experts use little jobbers made of twisted glass. These trinkets are called fermentation locks and may be purchased from shops specializing in wine making supplies. I use the cheaper and easily obtainable five cent balloon. The balloon is merely fit over the mouth of the jug. If the balloon begins to fill too rapidly, prick a small hole in the end of it to allow some of the gas to escape.

Fermentation

The fermentation process takes from two to four months. Little bubbles can be seen sliding up the sides of the jugs. When the bubbles stop rising, fermentation has ceased.

Sometimes a jelly-like substance forms in the jugs. This is often caused by pectin in the juice. To correct this, carefully strain the juice into a clean crock through several layers of cheese cloth. Discard jelly-like substance and return fermenting juice to clean jug. Boil water with an equal amount of sugar. Cool. Add sugar water to the jug to bring up original juice level.

After a week or so a white substance begins forming in the bottom of the jug. Don't panic! The substance is dead yeast cells and sediment separating from the liquid.

Siphoning

When fermentation stops, the yeast has converted the sugar into alcohol. The dead yeast cells have collected on the bottom of the jug along with other sediment. The wine must now be siphoned into clean sterilized jugs, leaving the dead cells and sediment behind.

A piece of surgical-rubber tubing makes an excellent siphon hose. Place the clean jug at a level lower than the full jug. Remove the balloon (or fermentation lock, if you were one of those enthusiastic individuals who had to rush out and buy one), insert one end of the hose into the wine. Suck gently on the other end to begin wine flow, then insert that end into clean jug. Be careful not to allow sediment to enter siphon hose. Use boiled, cooled water to replace volume lost to sediment, bringing wine level to one inch from the opening of the jug.

The jugs must now be sealed with sterilized caps or lids. Caps from used jugs may be utilized. Seal seam around caps with melted paraffin.

The wine will now begin to clear. More sediment will collect in the bottom of the jug. After approximately three months, siphon wine off sediment into clean jugs. If wine is clear at this point, it is ready to bottle. But most likely the wine will have to be left in the clean and sealed jugs another three months to clear.

Bottling

If your wine is red and you wish to preserve its color, bottle it in green glass. If the wine is white, clear glass is fine. Used wine bottles are excellent to use as long as they are not chipped or cracked. All bottles must be sterilized.

Corks should be prepared by soaking them in boiled water for twenty-four hours. Place the corks in hot water and weight them down with a heavy pot lid or plate so that they remain submerged. Always use new corks. Recycled corks can ruin the wine.

Carefully siphon wine from jugs into sterilized bottles, filling to one inch from the top. With a rubber mallet (or hammer cushioned in a rag) tap the corks into place. Label bottles. Don't forget to include the bottling date.

Aging

Wine should be aged and stored in a cool dark place.

Wine matures at different rates, depending on the ingredients used in their preparation. The following recipes estimate maturing time. However, large quantities of home made wines are consumed long before they get the chance to reach maturity.

Chapter II

Wild Berry Wines

BLACKBERRY WINE

There are numerous varieties of blackberries growing along fences, open woods, and uncultivated ground throughout North America. Blackberries are not only common, but make excellent wine. Wine produced from these berries matures quickly and is usually ready to consume in three months.

4 lbs. blackberries
2 gallons water
3 Tbsp. freshly squeezed lemon juice
2½ lbs. sugar
1 tsp. active dry yeast (if needed)

Place berries in crock; add water and mash berries. Cover and allow to sit for three days. Strain juice. Remove ½ gallon of juice to kettle and heat to boiling. Add sugar and stir until sugar dissolves. Add lemon juice and return sugar-juice mixture to crock.

Cover crock and allow to stand three days. If fermentation hasn't begun, add yeast. Pour blackberry mixture into jugs, fit with balloons and allow to work until action ceases. Carefully siphon into clean jugs and cap tightly. After three months, bottle wine; cork.

Wine should be mature in three months and ready to sample.

BLACKBERRY WINE

4 gallons ripe blackberries
1 gallon water
8 lbs. sugar

Place berries in crock. Boil water, then pour over berries in crock. Crush fruit. Cover and allow to stand for 48 hours, stirring occasionally.
Strain off juice and add sugar. Stir to dissolve sugar. Cover crock with loose fitting cover and allow to ferment until all action ceases. Carefully siphon into bottles; cork. Allow to mature 3 months.

BLACKCAP WINE

The blackcap vine is a low growing, thorny, creeper fround growing on rock slides, bluffs, and in gravel ladened soil. The berries are smaller than those of the blackberry and not easily found in quantity. However, blackcaps make one of the best berry wines. It's well worth harvesting!

4 gallons blackcaps
1 gallon water
6 gallons sugar
1 tsp. active dry yeast

Mash berries in crock, then cover with 1 gallon boiling water. Allow to steep for 24 hours, stirring occasionally. Strain juice, squeezing pulp as dry as possible. Discard pulp.
Add sugar to juice, stirring to dissolve, then stir in yeast. Cover crock. After violent action has ceased (1 to 2 weeks) siphon into jugs and fit with balloons. After 3 months, siphon into bottles; cork. Blackcap wine will be ready for sampling in 4 to 6 weeks.

BLUEBERRY WINE

There are many species of blueberries scattered throughout the United States and Canada. The bushes vary from one to eleven feet in height and bear purple-black fruit with a grayish powdery coating. Though cultivated berries often grow nearly an inch in diameter, the wild varieties seldom obtain a size larger than a pea.

Juice of 6 oranges
½ lb. sugar
1 tsp. active dry yeast
7 pints blueberries
6 pints warm water
2½ lbs. sugar

Combine orange juice with ½ lb. sugar and yeast. Cover and set aside in warm place. Meanwhile, place fruit in crock and crush. Add warm water and allow to stand 24 hours, stirring occasionally. Strain juice, squeezing pulp as dry as possible. Discard pulp.

Return juice to crock. Add 2½ lbs. sugar. Stir in orange juice-yeast mixture. Cover crock with clean cloth and allow yeast to work until most action ceases (2 to 4 weeks). Siphon into jugs and fit with balloon. Allow to stand two months. Remove balloon and cap tightly.

After three months, carefully siphon wine into bottles; cork. Wine will be ready to sample in six months.

CROWBERRY WINE

The fruit of the crowberry is commonly used by the Indians of British Columbia and the Alaskan Eskimos. The glossy black berries are approximately ¼" in diameter and are found growing down amongst the tangled foliage of the shurb. Crowberry wine has a great deal of body and a delicate, yet distinct flavor.

5 lbs. crowberries
1 gallon water
¼ cup freshly squeezed lemon juice
1 compressed cake yeast, crumbled

Place berries in crock. Bring water to boil and pour over berries. Crush berries well. Cover crock with clean cloth and allow to stand 5 days, stirring twice daily. Strain liquid; discard pulp.

Add lemon juice and sugar. Sprinkle yeast over surface and stir well. Cover crock and allow to stand three days. Siphon liquid into jugs and fit with balloon. Allow container to remain undisturbed until action ceases (approximately 6 weeks).

Siphon into clean containers, avoiding sediment. Cap containers and allow to rest three months. Carefully siphon into clean bottles; cork.

Wine will be ready for the table in twelve months.

WILD CURRANT WINE

There are dozens of different types of wild currants growing throughout the United States and Canada. The best wild currant for winemaking is the red Squaw Currant. Some winemakers mix together several varieties of currants found growing in neighboring areas and obtain excellent results.

6 lbs. wild currants
1 gallon water
3 lbs. sugar
1 tsp. active dry yeast

Place currants in crock. Boil water and pour over berries in crock. Allow to soak for three days, mashing and stirring daily. Strain juice and discard pulp.

Add sugar, cover crock and allow to stand four days. If action has not begun, add yeast. Ladle into jugs and fit with balloons. Allow to remain undisturbed until action ceases.

Siphon into clean containers, cap tightly and allow to rest three to four months. Strain into clean containers and allow to rest three months longer. Carefully siphon into bottles; cork.

Matures in six months.

WILD CURRANT WINE (dessert)

5 lbs. wild currants (stems removed)
7 gallons water
4 lbs. honey
9 lbs. sugar
2 egg whites
1 oz. cream of tartar

Press juice from currants; discarding solids. Boil together water and honey; cool to lukewarm, then pour into crock, along with currant juice. Stir well. Cover crock with clean cloth and allow to stand four days.

Add sugar to crock; stir well. Beat together egg whites and cream of tartar. Stir mixture into liquid. Siphon into jugs and fit with balloon. After 4 months, siphon into bottles; cork.

Allow wine to age at least 6 months before serving.

DEWBERRY WINE

The oblong, black dewberries are a form of blackberry, but are easier to harvest since their thorns are more widely scattered. Wine made from dewberries have a flavor similar to blackberry wine.

3 gallons ripe dewberries
1 gallon warm water
6 lbs. sugar
1 tsp. active dry yeast

Place berries in crock and cover with warm water. Crush fruit. Cover crock and allow to stand for three days, stirring daily.

Strain juice, squeezing pulp as dry as possible. Add sugar to juice and stir to dissolve. Add yeast. Cover crock with clean cloth and allow to stand five days.

Siphon juice into jugs and fit with balloon. After seven weeks, remove balloons and cap jugs. Three months later, siphon into bottles; cork.

Matures in three months.

ELDERBERRY WINE

Elderberries thrive in damp places in woods and valleys, and along streams and rivers throughout most of North America. The large clusters of bluish-black colored berries ripen during the fall. It is best to harvest the berries after the first frost, since this is when their flavor peaks.

4 lbs. elderberries (stripped from their stems)
2 gallons water
2 cups raisins
1 - 1" piece fresh ginger root
1 lemon
3 lbs. sugar
1 tsp. active dry yeast

Place berries and raisins in kettle along with two gallons of water. Bring to boiling and simmer for 10 minutes. Strain juice. Squeeze juice from lemon and add to berry juice, along with sugar and bruised ginger; simmer 10 minutes. Strain juice through several layers of cheese cloth, then pour juice into clean crock. Allow juice to stand 48 hours, then decide whether yeast needs to be added.

After fermentation begins, allow to stand in crock for two weeks before siphoning fermenting liquid into clean jugs. Fit jugs with balloon and allow to stand undisturbed three months. Remove balloon and siphon juice into clean jugs. Cap tightly. Repeat siphoning three months later. Bottle and cork.

Matures in three to five years.

ELDERBERRY WINE (Dessert)

5 gallons elderberries (stems removed)
5 gallons warm water
20 lbs. sugar

Place berries and water in crock. Cover crock with clean cloth and allow to stand ten days, stirring daily. Strain juice through several layers of cheese cloth. Do not squeeze or crush berries. Discard solids.

Add sugar to elderberry liquid. Cover crock with clean cloth and allow to stand until active fermentation has ceased (three to four weeks). Cover crock opening with plastic wrap and secure tightly in place with elastic or rubber hose. Allow to rest two months before siphoning into bottles. Cork.

Matures in three years.

SPICED ELDERBERRY WINE

4 gallons elderberries (stems removed)
2 gallons water
6 lbs. sugar
3 oz. whole cloves
3 oz. sliced ginger root
2 tsp. active dry yeast

Place berries in crock and cover with two gallons of boiling water. Allow to steep for 24 hours, stirring occasionally. Strain liquid through several layers of cheese cloth, squeezing out as much juice as possible Discard pulp.

Add sugar and spices to juice, pour into kettle and simmer for 20 minutes, skimming constantly. Cool to lukewarm, strain juice, discarding spices, and add yeast. Cover crock. After four days, siphon fermenting juice into jugs and fit with balloon. Siphon into bottles, after four months, and cork.

Matures in two to three years.

EUROPEAN RED HAWTHORNE WINE

The European Red Hawthorn is commonly found along ditch banks and vacant lots. The abundant berries cling to the bush throughout much of the winter. Wine made from these berries should be bottled in green glass to protect the rich rose color.

8 pints European Red Hawthorn berries
1 gallon water
2 oranges
3 lbs. sugar
2 Tbsp. strong tea
1 tsp. active dry yeast
1 tsp. cream of tartar

Crush hawthorn berries with mallot, then dump into crock. Pour one gallon of boiling water over fruit. Grate orange rind into crock; squeeze orange and add juice to fruit in crock. Allow crock to stand covered for two days.

Add sugar and tea to crock. Let liquid stand in open crock another day before adding yeast and cream of tartar. Place crock in warm place and let liquid work for four days.

Strain liquid through pillow case; discard solids. Siphon into jugs and fit with balloons. Allow to work six to eight weeks.

Siphon into clean jugs, cap and allow to rest for four months before carefully siphoning into clean jugs. Repeat siphoning in three months, this time siphoning into bottles. Cork.

Wine matures in eight months.

WILD GOOSEBERRY WINE

Wild gooseberries are found along stream banks and swampy areas. There are numerous varieties and all make pleasant wines. Gooseberry shrubs grow between two and five feet tall. The reddish to purple berries ripen during late summer.

5 lbs. wild gooseberries
1 gallon water
2½ lbs. sugar
1 tsp. active dry yeast

Place berries in crock. Boil water and pour over berries. Allow to soak for three days in covered crock. Carefully mash berries and allow to stand in covered crock two more days. Strain liquid into clean crock. Add sugar, then yeast.

Siphon into jugs and fit with balloons. Allow jugs to remain undisturbed until action ceases. Siphon into clean jugs and cap tightly. After four months, carefully siphon into bottles. Cork.

Allow to mature at least two years.

WILD GRAPE WINE

Over half the world's wild grapes are native to this country. Some two dozen species are scattered across the United States. The flavor of wild grapes range from extremely tart to sweet, therefore, producing wines with a great deal of flavor variance. Wild species noted for their wine are fox grapes, the scuppernong, pigeon grapes, and the native muscadine.

Other species offer fine wines also, and are worth experiencing.

1 bushel wild grapes (fully ripe)
1½ gallons warm water
16 lbs. sugar

Pour warm water over grapes in crock. Mash fruit, being careful not to break seeds. Cover crock and allow to stand for seven to eight days, stirring daily.

Strain juice into clean crock, using pillow case. Discard solids. Stir in sugar and allow to stand in warm place until fermentation begins. Cover crock and allow to stand in warm place for four to five weeks, stirring occasionally.

Siphon juice into clean jugs and fit with balloons. After four months, carefully siphon wine into clean bottles; cork.

Matures in one year, but is better if left longer.

WILD GRAPE WINE (Sparkling)

15 lbs. wild grapes (partially ripened)
2½ gallons water
9 lbs. sugar
2 oz. cream of tartar

Place grapes and water in crock. Mash well, then cover crock with clean cloth and allow to stand for 48 hours. Strain juice into clean crock, using pillow case. Squeeze pulp as dry as possible, then discard solids.

Add sugar and cream of tartar to juice. Stir well. Allow mixture to stand, covered, for six to seven days. Stir well, then cover and allow to stand four to five months.

Siphon wine into bottles; cork.

Matures in eight months.

WILD GRAPE WINE (Dessert)

1 bushel wild grapes (fully ripened)
13 lbs. sugar
2 gallons grape brandy
2 gallons water

Remove all stems from grapes and place fruit in crock. Mash grapes well, being careful not to crush seeds. Add sugar, brandy, and water. Cover with clean cloth and allow to stand for seven days, stirring daily.

Strain juice, through pillow case, into clean crock. Allow sediment to settle for three days before carefully siphoning juice into jugs. Fit with balloons. After three months, siphon into bottles; cork.

Wine is ready for sampling in eight to twelve months.

SPICED WILD GRAPE WINE

15 lbs. fully ripened wild grapes
2 gallons water
8 lbs. sugar
4 oz. cloves
3 oz. sliced ginger root
3 oz. stick cinnamon
1 tsp. active dry yeast

Place grapes in crock and cover with two gallons boiling water. Mash fruit gently, being careful not to break seeds. Allow to stand 48 hours, stirring occasionally. Strain liquid through pillow case, squeezing out as much juice as possible. Discard pulp.

Pour juice into large kettle; add sugar and spices. Heat kettle over medium heat until boiling, reduce heat and simmer 15 minutes, skimming occasionally. Strain juice, discarding spices. Cool, then add yeast.

After yeast has been working for seven days, ladle fermenting liquid into jugs and fit with balloons. Allow to work in jugs until action ceases.

Siphon into clean jugs and cap tightly. After four months, siphon into bottles; cork.

Allow wine to mature at least eight months.

HIGHBUSH CRANBERRY WINE

Highbush cranberries grow on tall shrubs, ripening during late summer. It is not difficult to gather a sufficient supply for winemaking. Wine made from these berries has a delicate red hue and tart flavor.

7 lbs. highbush cranberries
1 gallon water
4 lbs. sugar
2 cups freshly squeezed orange juice
1½ tsp. active dry yeast

Dissolve yeast in orange juice. Place mixture in jar, cover, and store in warm place.

Place berries in crock. Boil water and pour over berries. Allow fruit to soak for three days, mashing and stirring daily. Strain into clean crock through pillow case. Discard pulp.

Stir sugar into juice, then add orange juice-yeast mixture. Stir gently, then siphon juice into jugs. Fit jugs with balloons and allow juice to work until action ceases.

Siphon into clean containers, cap tightly and allow to rest three months. Again siphon into clean jugs. Allow to rest three months longer. Carefully siphon into bottles. Cork.

Matures in eight to ten months.

HUCKLEBERRY WINE

Huckleberries are usually found growing along mountain slopes. These low, highly branched shrubs produce one of the most sought after wild fruits of the Northwest. The bluish-black berries ripen during late July through early September. Huckleberries produce one of the finest wild wines.

1 pint orange juice
½ lb. sugar
1 tsp. active dry yeast
5 pints huckleberries
2 lbs. sugar

Combine ½ lb. sugar with orange juice. Add yeast and set aside in warm place.

In crock, cursh fruit. Add 2 quarts water which has been boiled to room temperature. Let stand, covered, for 24 hours. Squeeze juice through several layers of cheese cloth or pillow case, into clean crock. Discard pulp.

Boil 1 lb. sugar in ¼ gallon water for 1 minute. Cool. Mix with juice, along with half orange juice-yeast mixture. Allow to ferment for two weeks in crock covered with clean cloth.

Boil 1 lb. sugar in remaining water. Allow to cool. Add to huckleberry liquid along with remaining orange juice-yeast mixture. Transfer liquid into jugs and fit with balloon. Leave in warm place until action ceases. Siphon into bottles; cork.

Matures in six months.

LOGANBERRY WINE

Loganberries have naturalized in British Columbia, Oregon, Washington, and Northern California. The bushes bear fruit during June, July, and August. Wine made from the fruit is one of the more popular.

>   6 lbs. loganberries
>   1 gallon water
>   2 tsp. cream of tartar
>   3 lbs. sugar
>   1 tsp. active dry yeast

Place berries and water in crock. Mash well, then cover crock with a clean cloth and allow to stand for three days. Strain juice and squeeze pulp as dry as possible; discard solids.
Add cream of tartar and sugar to juice. Stir well. Add yeast and allow mixture to stand in open crock for two days, then siphon into jugs and fit with balloons. When action ceases, siphon into clean jug; cap. Allow wine to clear for four months before siphoning into bottles. Cork.
Loganberry wine is at its best when allowed to age at least eight months.

SPICED LOGANBERRY WINE

>   4 gallons ripe loganberries
>   1 oz. cloves
>   1 oz. stick cinnamon
>   4 lbs. sugar
>   1 gallon warm water

Place berries in crock and cover with water. Add spices. Cover crock and allow to stand four days, stirring daily.
Add sugar. Cover crock and allow to stand two weeks. Strain into clean crock, discarding solids. Cover and allow to stand until fermentation ceases (4 to 6 weeks). Siphon into bottles. Cork.
Matures in four to six months.

MOUNTAIN ASH WINE

The brilliant orange mountain ash berries are harvested after frost has formed. At this point, the fruit begins to ferment on the bush. Be certain all stems and leaves have been removed from the berries before they are placed in the crock.

8 pints mountain ash berries
1½ gallons hot water
2 oranges
1 lemon
3½ lbs. sugar
1 tsp. active dry yeast
2 Tbsp. strong tea

Crush berries with mallet, then dump into crock. Cover berries with hot water. Put oranges and lemons through food grinder. Add fruit to crock. Cover with lid or clean cloth and let stand one week.

Strain liquid through pillow case. Discard solids. Add sugar and yeast. Cover crock and allow to stand five days.

Siphon juice into clean jugs and fit with balloon. After action ceases (4 to 6 weeks) siphon into clean jugs, add tea, and cap tightly. After four months, siphon into bottles; cork.

Matures in two years.

MOUNTAIN CRANBERRY WINE

Mountain cranberries grow on drier forest floors, whereas the bog cranberries thrive in damp sphagnum. Either cranberry makes excellent wine.

4 lbs. wild cranberries
2 gallons boiling water
10 lbs. sugar
4 cups freshly squeezed orange juice
1 tsp. active dry yeast

Place cranberries in crock; cover with boiling water. Mash berries. Cover crock and allow to stand for five days. Meanwhile, in jar, mix yeast with orange juice plus two cups sugar. Set aside in warm place.

Strain juice into clean crock. Discard solids. Stir in yeast mixture and remaining sugar. Cover crock and allow to stand two days before siphoning into clean jugs. Fit with balloons. After four months, siphon into clean jugs; cap. Three months later, siphon into bottles; cork.

Matures in eight to ten months.

OREGON GRAPE WINE

Oregon grape is an evergreen shrub with holly-like leaves. It thrives in woods and dry open areas from British Columbia to California. It is especially abundant west of the Cascade Mountains. Berries are blue with a white powdery coating. Wine made from Oregon grape berries has a slightly musky flavor many find pleasing.

3 lbs. Oregon grape berries
1 gallon water
2½ lbs. sugar
Juice of 1 lemon
1 tsp. active dry yeast

Place berries in crock and crush with small wooden mallet. Boil water and pour over fruit. Cover crock and allow pulp to stand for four days, stirring daily. Strain liquid into clean crock; discard solids.

Remove ½ gallon extracted juice to saucepan and heat to boiling. Stir in sugar and lemon juice. Remove from heat and allow to cool. Return cooled liquid to crock and add yeast. Cover crock and allow liquid to ferment until action ceases. Carefully siphon liquid into jugs and cap tightly.

After three months, siphon into clean bottles; cork.

Allow wine to age between eighteen and twenty-four months.

RED HUCKLEBERRY WINE

Red huckleberries grow on high bushes and are easily spotted throughout the Pacific Northwest. Wine made from this fruit has a splendid flavor and clean, light red color.

6 lbs. wild huckleberries
1 gallon water
3½ lbs. sugar
1 pint freshly squeezed orange juice
1 tsp. active dry yeast

Place berries in crock, mash berries, then cover with water. Cover crock and allow to stand five days. Meanwhile, in jar, combine two cups sugar, orange juice and yeast. Set aside.

Strain juice into clean crock; discard solids. Add sugar. Stir in yeast-orange juice mixture. Siphon into jugs and fit with balloons. After action ceases, siphon into clean jugs and cap tightly. After four months, carefully siphon into bottles; cork.

Matures in six months.

RED MULBERRY WINE

The mulberry is common in the warm climate areas of the United States. The berries resemble soft blackberries and range from deep red to black in color. The mulberry has been a popular wine fruit for centuries. Harvest berries just as they are turning from red to black.

3 gallons crushed mulberries
3 gallons water
15 lbs. sugar

Pour water over crushed berries in crock; allow to stand uncovered for 48 hours. Strain juice through several layers of cheese cloth or pillow case, squeezing pulp as dry as possible.

Add sugar to juice, cover crock and allow to stand until the most active part of fermentation ceases.

Siphon into clean jugs and fit with balloons. After four months, siphon into clean bottles; cork.

Matures in six months.

WILD RED RASPBERRY WINE

Wild raspberries thrive in areas where summers are cool. They prefer rich soil and moderate moisture. Wine made from wild raspberries has qualities similar to those found in wine commercially made from cultivated raspberries.

5 gallons ripe wild raspberries
1 gallon water
5 lbs. sugar

Place berries in crock. Crush berries, then add water. Cover crock with clean cloth or lid and allow to stand for five days.

Add sugar. Cover and allow to stand one week. Strain juice into clean crock; discard solids. Siphon juice into clean jugs and fit with balloons. After action ceases, siphon into clean jugs and cap tightly. Four months later, siphon into bottles; cork.

Matures in five months.

WILD ROSE HIP WINE

Wild rose hips, the fruit of the wild rose, ripens in the fall. The red to orange-red fruits can be gathered during the winter since they remain on the bush throughout the season. Dried rose hips are available at most natural food stores and may be used in place of fresh or frozen. Use three cups dried hips, when substituting for fresh, for each pound of fresh rose hips.

5 lbs. rose hips
1 lb. raisins
2 lemons
1 gallon water
3½ lbs. sugar
1 tsp. active dry yeast

Wash rose hips. With food grinder, grind together rose hips, raisins and lemons. Dump ground fruit into crock. Cover fruit in crock with boiling water. Cover crock and allow to stand for four days.
  Strain liquid into clean crock; discard solids. Add sugar. Sprinkle yeast over surface of liquid, then cover crock and allow to stand four days.
  Siphon fermenting liquid into jugs and fit with balloons. After action ceases, siphon into clean jugs and cap tightly. Repeat procedure three more times at three month intervals, being careful to avoid sediment in bottom of jugs.
  Siphon wine into bottles; cork.
  Wine will be ready for the table in eight months.

SPICED WILD ROSE HIP WINE

4 lbs. ripe wild rose hips
1 lemon, thinly sliced
1½ Tbsp. whole cloves
3 cinnamon sticks
3 lbs. sugar
1 gallon water
1 tsp. active dry yeast

Wash hips well; crush with mallet and place fruit in crock. Pour over ¼ gallon of water. Boil 1½ lbs. sugar in 1 quart water for two minutes. Cool ten minutes, then add lemon and spices. Add sugar-water to fruit, mix well.

Add yeast and cover crock with clean cloth or lid. Allow to ferment one week. Strain liquid into clean crock; discard solids. Boil 1½ lbs. sugar in three quarts of water for four minutes. Cool twenty minutes, then add to rose hip liquor.

Allow liquor to ferment another week. Strain, then pour into jugs and fit with balloons. Leave jugs undisturbed until action ceases (4 to 6 weeks). Siphon into clean bottles; cork.

Matures in six to eight months.

SALAL WINE

Salal is found west of the Cascade Mountains and along the coast from Alaska to California. Fleshy black berries grow along the stems of this evergreen shrub, ripening in late August. Wine from the salal berries has an aromatic fragrance. Some individuals find salal wine to be too mild in flavor, however, and opt to mix it with equal amounts of a stronger flavored wine. Salal wine is a good project for the novice winemaker since the berries are abundant and easily harvested.

4 lbs. salal berries (stems removed)
1 gallon water
2 Tbsp. lemon juice
2½ lbs. sugar
½ lb. ground raisins
1 tsp. active dry yeast

Place berries in crock. Bring water to boil and pour over berries. Crush berries slightly, cover crock, and allow to rest for four to five days, stirring once daily. Strain liquid into clean crock, discarding solids. Add lemon juice and sugar, then yeast and raisins. Pour fermenting liquid into jugs and fit with balloons. Allow containers to stand undisturbed until action ceases.

Siphon liquid into clean jugs, avoiding sediment. Cap jugs and allow wine to settle for three months. Carefully siphon into bottles; cork.

Wine will be ready for the table in ten to twelve months.

SPICED SALAL WINE

5 lbs. salal berries (stems removed)
1 lemon, thinly sliced
1 orange, thinly sliced
2 Tbsp. whole cloves
4 cinnamon sticks
2½ lbs. sugar
1 gallon water
1 tsp. active dry yeast

Place berries in crock and mash well. Pour over ¼ gallon of water. Boil 1 lb. sugar in 1 quart water for two minutes; cool ten minutes. Tie cloves and cinnamon in square of cheese cloth and place in crock. Pour over sugar-water. Add lemon and orange. Mix well.

Add yeast and cover crock. Allow to ferment one week. Strain liquid into clean crock; discard solids. Boil 1½ lbs. sugar in three quarts water for two minutes. Cool twenty minutes, then add to liquid in crock.

Allow to ferment one week longer, then siphon liquid into jugs. Fit with balloons and leave undisturbed until action ceases. Siphon into clean jugs and cap tightly. Allow wine to clear for three months before siphoning into clean bottles. Cork.

Matures in eight to ten months.

SALMONBERRY WINE

The mild-flavored salmonberry is found growing along creeks and in moist places west of the Cascade Mountains from Alaska to California. Salmonberries are orange or red and resemble large juicy raspberries. Since the berries begin ripening in June, Salmonberry wine can be ready to sample by Thanksgiving.

3 gallons crushed salmonberries
2 gallons water
8 lbs. sugar

Pour water over berries in crock. Crush well, then cover crock and let stand five days. Stir in sugar. Cover crock and allow to stand one week longer.

Strain juice through pillow case, squeezing pulp as dry as possible. Discard solids. Return juice to clean crock, cover, and allow to stand three days. Siphon into jugs and fit with balloons. Allow to stand in jugs three months before siphoning into bottles; cork.

Matures in three months.

SEA GRAPE WINE

Sea grapes grow in the semi-tropical areas along the Gulf of Mexico. Wildcrafters have gathered the fruit for use in pies and jams. Sea grapes also make exciting wine!

2 gallons sea grapes
1 gallon water
3 lbs. sugar
1 tsp. active dry yeast

Place sea grapes and water in large kettle. Heat and crush fruit over medium heat until temperature of juice reaches 165°F. Promptly remove from heat; cool fruit slightly before pouring into clean crock. Cover crock with lid or clean cloth and let pulp soak for five days.

Strain juice into clean crock through pillow case; discard solids. Stir in sugar, then add yeast. Cover crock and let liquid work until fermenting ceases. Carefully siphon liquid into jugs and cap tightly. Allow to stand three months before siphoning wine into bottles; cork.

Wine matures in eight months, but improves with age.

SERVICEBERRY WINE

The adaptable serviceberry ranges from sea level to approximately 7,500 feet above sea level. Early pioneers used the berries to mix with pounded dried buffalo meat for pemmican. However, the flavor of these plump, juicy berries would be better represented as an after dinner wine.

6 lbs. serviceberries (stems removed)
2 Tbsp. grated orange rind
1 gallon water
3 lbs. sugar
3 cups freshly squeezed orange juice
1 tsp. active dry yeast

Place berries and grated orange rind in crock. Mash well, then cover with one gallon water. Stir, then cover crock and allow to stand for four days.

Meanwhile, mix together orange juice, two cups sugar and yeast. Set aside in warm place.

Strain serviceberry liquid into clean crock; discard solids. Add remaining sugar, then stir in yeast mixture. Siphon into jugs and fit with balloons. After action ceases, siphon into clean jugs and cap tightly. Repeat siphoning procedure again after four months. Allow wine to stand three months, then bottle. Cork.

Matures in nine to twelve months.

SUMACH WINE

Sumach is a common native shrub which bears a conical cluster of tiny, hairy, dark-red berries during later summer. The shrub thrives in dry interior valleys throughout the United States. The fruit is easily gathered by rubbing the berries off the stalk and discarding the stem. Wine produced from sumach has a distinct, tart flavor.

It is important to know which sumach varieties are edible as some Eastern varieties are thought to be poisonous.

1 pint orange juice
1 tsp. active dry yeast
5 lbs. sumach berries
2 gallons water
3 lbs. sugar

Combine ½ lb. sugar with orange juice. Add yeast and set aside in warm place.

Place fruit in crock and crush berries. Add two quarts of water which has been boiled, then cooled to room temperature. Let stand tightly covered for 24 hours. Squeeze juice into clean crock through pillow case. Discard pulp.

Boil 1 lb. sugar in ½ gallon water for one minutes. Cool. Mix with juice, along with half orange juice-yeast mixture. Allow to ferment for two weeks in crock covered with clean cloth. Strain liquid through several layers of cheese cloth. Boil ½ lb. sugar in remaining water. Allow to cool. Add to berry liquid, along with remaining orange juice-yeast mixture. Transfer liquid into jugs and fit with balloons. After action ceases, siphon into clean jugs and cap tightly. Siphon into bottles three months later, being careful to avoid sediment at the bottom of the jug. Cork.

Matures in nine months.

THIMBLEBERRY WINE

The erect, thornless thimbleberry shrub is found throughout the Northwest from sea level to elevations of 8,000 feet. Bright red, bowl-shaped berries ripen during late July and early August.

It is difficult to find large quantities of thimbleberries, but for individuals favoring a delicate, light-bodied wine, the berries are well worth seeking.

4 gallons thimbleberries
1 gallon water
4 lbs. sugar
1 tsp. active dry yeast

Place berries in crock. Mash well before adding water. Cover crock with clean cloth or lid and allow to stand four days. Add sugar and allow to stand two weeks longer.

Strain juice through pillow case, squeezing pulp as dry as possible. Discard solids. Cover crock and allow to stand for five days. If liquid begins to ferment, omit yeast. Otherwise, stir yeast into liquid.

Siphon liquid into jugs and fit with balloons. After six to eight weeks, siphon into clean jugs and cap tightly. Four months later, carefully siphon into bottles. Cork.

Matures in three months.

Chapter III

Wild Flower Wine

ROADSIDE APPLE BLOSSOM WINE

Roadside or wild apples bloom profusely during May. The sweet scented blossoms make a delicate, fragrant wine. Roadside Apple Blossom Wine is excellent when blended with a full-bodied berry wine.

> *1 gallon apple blossoms (just petals and stamens)*
> *2 oranges*
> *2 lemons*
> *1 gallon water*
> *2½ lbs. sugar*
> *1 tsp. active dry yeast*
> *1 tsp. strong tea*

Place blossoms in crock along with thinly pared rinds of oranges and lemons. Bring water to boil and pour over blossoms and rind, crushing and stirring to extract flavor. Cover crock and leave for four to five days, stirring twice daily.

Strain liquid, pressing pulp to extract as much moisture as possible. Discard solids.

Add sugar, juice of lemons and oranges, and yeast. Stir well, then siphon into clean jugs. Fit with balloons. When fermentation ceases, ciphon liquid into clean jugs, add tea and cap tightly.

After three months, carefully siphon wine into bottles. Cork. Matures in eight months.

CAMOMILE WINE

Camomile is a small flowering plant which flourishes in meadows, pastures, vacant lots, and along roadsides. It is best known for its use in herb tea, but makes a fine wine, also. Dried camomile blossoms can be purchased at natural food stores and may be used in place of freshly gathered flowers. Use ⅔ of a gallon of dried blossoms when substituting for fresh.

>1½ gallons comomile blossoms
>1 gallon water
>3 oranges
>1 large lemon
>2¾ lbs. sugar
>1 tsp. active dry yeast
>1½ tsp. strong tea

Place blossoms in large kettle along with one gallon of water. Place over medium heat and bring to a boil. Promptly remove kettle from heat and pour contents into clean crock. Cover crock and allow to steep for four to five days, stirring occasionally.

Strain liquid into clean crock, discarding pulp. Add sugar, juice from oranges and lemon, and yeast. Stir well before siphoning liquid into jugs. Fit with balloons.

After action ceases, siphon into clean jugs with tight fitting caps and allow liquid to remain undisturbed for three months. Siphon liquid into clean jugs, cap, and allow to stand three months longer. Carefully siphon into bottles; cork.

Allow to mature at least eight months.

COWSLIP WINE

The cowslip, or marsh marigold, ranges from the Carolinas to the Arctic. It blooms among meadows during early spring. Cowslip wine is one of the most flavorful of the wild blossom wines.

3 pints cowslip blossoms, lightly packed
  (no green parts or stems)
1 gallon boiling water
3 lbs. sugar
2 lemons, ground
1 tsp. cream of tartar
1 cup orange juice
1 tsp. active dry yeast

Place cowslip blossoms in crock and cover with one gallon boiling water. Add sugar and ground lemon. Cover crock and allow to stand for four days, stirring daily.

Meanwhile, stir yeast into orange juice and set aside in a warm place. After four days, strain liquid into clean crock; discard solids. Add orange juice-yeast mixture to strained liquid. Stir in cream of tartar. Siphon into jugs and fit with balloons.

After three months, siphon into clean jugs and cap tightly. Siphon again three months later. At the end of three months, siphon into bottles. Cork.

Wine is now ready to sample, but improves with age.

WILD DAISY WINE

Wild Daisy Wine is a good project for the novice winemaker because daisies are not only abundant and easily gathered, but also make wine which matures quickly.

> *2 gallons wild daisy heads (all green parts and stems removed)*
> *2 gallons warm water*
> *6 lbs. sugar*
> *1 tsp. active dry yeast*

Place blossoms in crock and cover with two gallons warm water. Cover crock and allow to stand for three days. Strain liquid into a clean crock, squeezing pulp as dry as possible; discard solids.

Add sugar and yeast to strained liquid. Allow liquid to work in crock three weeks before siphoning into jugs. Fit jugs with balloons and allow to stand for three months. Siphon into bottles, being careful to leave sediment behind. Cork.

Wine is now ready to be served.

DANDELION WINE

The common, world-wide weed is easily harvested from lawns, fields, gardens, and roadsides. It produces one of the finest flower wines.

>1½ gallons fresh dandelion petals
>   (no stems or green parts)
>8 sliced oranges
>4 sliced lemons
>1 gallon water
>2½ lbs. sugar

Place blossoms and fruit in crock. Boil one gallon of water and pour over ingredients in crock. Stir well, then cover crock and let stand for 24 hours. Strain liquid, squeezing pulp as dry as possible. Discard solids.
Return liquid to clean crock and add sugar. Cover crock and allow to stand two weeks, stirring occasionally. Skim scum from surface of liquid, cover crock and allow to stand two weeks longer.
After three months, siphon into bottles; cork.
Matures in eight months.

DANDELION WINE (Dessert)

>1 gallon lightly packed dandelion petals
>   (no stems or green parts)
>1 gallon water
>4 lbs. sugar
>½ cup brandy
>1 tsp. active dry yeast

Place blossoms in crock and pour one gallon of boiling water over dandelions. Let steep for five days, then strain, pressing blossoms as dry as possible. Discard solids.
Return liquid to crock and add sugar, brandy, and yeast. Cover crock and allow to ferment one week before skimming surface. Siphon into jugs and fit with balloons. When wine is clear, siphon into bottles; cork.
Dandelion wine should age at least eight months.

DOGWOOD BLOSSOM WINE

The beautiful spring blooming dogwood is a familiar sight throughout much of North America. Bring a breath of spring to the table during bleak winter months by serving Dogwood Blossom Wine.

1½ gallon dogwood petals
1 gallon hot water
1 lemon
2 oranges
3 lbs. sugar
1 tsp. active dry yeast
2 tsp. strong tea

Place petals in crock and cover with one gallon hot water. Put lemon and oranges through food chopper. Add to contents of crock. Cover crock and allow to stand four days.

Strain liquid through pillow case. Discard spent petals. Stir in sugar and yeast. Cover crock and allow to stand for four days before siphoning into jugs. Fit with balloons. After two to three months, remove balloons and cap jugs tightly. After three months, siphon into bottles; cork.

Matures in eight months.

ELDERFLOWER WINE

The blossoms of the blue elderberry are famous for the wine they produce. The flowers appear from late spring to early summer and are gathered just as they are ready to drop from the umbels by placing the umbels into a bag and shaking vigorously (be certain to pick out the bugs).

1 gallon elderflower blossoms
1 tsp. ground nutmeg
1 gallon boiling water
2½ lbs. sugar
1 cup freshly squeezed lemon juice
1 tsp. active dry yeast

Place blossoms and nutmeg in crock and cover with one gallon of boiling water. Add sugar and lemon juice. Stir well. Cover crock with clean cloth or lid and allow to stand one week.

Strain liquid through pillow case; discard solids. Allow strained liquid to stand, covered, two weeks. If action has not begun, add yeast. Siphon into jugs and fit with balloons. After action ceases, siphon into clean jugs and cap tightly. Repeat siphoning twice again at three month intervals. Bottle and cork.

Matures in eight months.

ELDERFLOWER WINE (Dessert)

3 quarts elderflowers
1 gallon boiling water
1 lb. honey
3 lbs. sugar
1 tsp. active dry yeast

Place flowers in crock and cover with boiling water. Stir in honey and sugar. Cover crock with clean cloth or lid and let stand for seven days.

Strain liquid through pillow case; discard pulp. Stir in yeast. Cover and let stand three days. Siphon into jugs and fit with balloons. Allow to stand until action ceases, then siphon into clean jugs and cap tightly. After four months, siphon into clean jugs. Three months later, siphon into bottles; cork.

Matures in six to eight months.

GOLDEN ROD WINE

There are over one hundred species of golden rod growing throughout North America. It thrives in the mountain areas, plains, swamps, dry fields, along waterways, roadsides and oceans. The bright yellow flower clusters have been used in winemaking for many years.

1 gallon packed golden rod blossoms
  (no green parts or stems)
1 gallon boiling water
2 oranges
1 lemon
3 lbs. sugar

Place blossoms in crock with boiling water. Run citrus fruit through food grinder and add to crock. Stir in sugar. Cover and allow to stand two weeks, stirring daily.

Strain liquid through pillow case, discarding solids. Cover crock and allow to stand one week. Remove scum from top of liquid and allow to stand, covered, another week. Skim again before siphoning into jugs. Fit jugs with balloons and allow to stand three months. Carefully siphon into clean jugs and cap tightly. Siphon again in three months. After three months, siphon into bottles; cork.

Matures in eight months.

HIBISCUS FLOWER WINE

The large flowered hibiscus grows wild in moist bottom lands of the southern United States and the Hawaiian Islands. This flower has a color range of light pink to purple. Red hibiscus flowers make a colorful wine which should be bottled in green glass to preserve its hue.

6 quarts hibiscus flowers
2 gallons water
2 lbs. sugar
1 lb. honey
½ cup freshly squeezed lemon juice
1 tsp. active dry yeast

Place blossoms in crock; pour over one gallon boiling water. Cover crock and allow to stand 48 hours.

Strain liquid into clean crock. Discard solids. Bring one gallon of water to boil and add sugar and honey. Simmer ten minutes. Remove from heat and allow to cool. Add strained hibiscus liquid and lemon juice. Stir in yeast. Siphon into jugs and fit with balloons. After action ceases, siphon liquid into clean jugs and cap tightly. Allow liquid to stand four months before siphoning into bottles. Cork.

Matures in eight months.

HONEYSUCKLE BLOSSOM WINE

Honeysuckle is most often found along sheltered embankments throughout the United States. Numerous native species offer a wide variety of color, ranging from yellow to purple. Wine made from honeysuckly blossoms has a sweet bouquet and mild flavor.

*1 gallon honeysuckle blossoms
   (no green stems or leaves)*
1 gallon water
2 oranges
1 large lemon
3 lbs. sugar
1 tsp. strong tea

Place blossoms in large kettle along with one gallon water. Place over medium heat and bring to a boil. Promptly remove from heat and pour into clean crock. Cover and allow to steep for two days, stirring occasionally. Strain liquid into clean crock, discarding pulp. Stir in sugar, juice from oranges and lemons, and yeast. Siphon into jugs and fit with balloons.

After action ceases, siphon into clean jugs, add tea, and cap tightly. Allow liquid to remain undisturbed for two months. Siphon liquid into clean jugs, being careful not to disturb sediment. After three months, siphon into bottles; cork.

Matures in ten months.

LAVENDAR BLOSSOM WINE

Lavender is a member of the mint family. Its fragrant flowers are best harvested from the shrub during June. Select a dry, warm afternoon for gathering blossoms since this is when the fragrance is at its peak.

2 gallons lavender blossoms
1½ gallons warm water
5 lbs. sugar
1 tsp. active dry yeast
2 cups freshly squeezed orange juice
1 cup honey

Place blossoms in crock and add water and sugar. Cover crock and allow to stand for two days. In jar, combine yeast, orange juice, and honey. Secure lid and shake vigorously.

Strain liquid through pillow case; discard solids. Add yeast mixture to strained liquid, cover crock and let stand for three days. Siphon into jugs and fit with balloons. After action ceases, siphon into clean jugs and fit with balloons. After action ceases, siphon into clean jugs and cap tightly. Siphon again in three months. Allow to stand four months before siphoning into bottles. Cork.

Matures in six to eight months.

MILKWEED BLOSSOM WINE

Milkweed can be found thriving along roadsides and fields from the Atlantic to the Pacific. Its sweet-smelling blossoms differ in color from a greenish-lilac shade to an off white.

It is important to use only the blossoms, since any green or stem parts contain a milky substance which produces a very disagreeable bitter flavor.

1 gallon milkweed blossoms
1 gallon boiling water
2 cups orange juice
1 lb. ground raisins
3 lbs. sugar
1 tsp. active dry yeast

Place blossoms in crock and cover with boiling water. Add orange juice and raisins. Cover crock and allow to stand for four days, stirring daily.

Strain liquid into clean crock; discard solids. Add sugar to strained liquid. Stir in yeast. Cover crock and allow to stand five days, stirring occasionally.

Skim scum from surface of liquid, then siphon into clean jugs and fit with balloons. When action ceases, remove balloons and cap bottles tightly. After four months, siphon into bottles; cork.

Matures in four to six months.

POMEGRANATE BLOSSOM WINE

The pomegranate produces fragrant waxy blossoms. Gather them on a dry day during mid-afternoon and use as soon as possible.

> 3 quarts pomegranate petals
> 1 gallon water
> 2½ lbs. sugar
> ⅔ cup freshly squeezed lemon juice
> 1 tsp. active dry yeast

Place blossoms in crock and cover with warm water. Crush blossoms in water to release fragrance. Cover crock with heavy lid and allow to stand for four days, stirring daily.

Strain liquid through pillow case, discarding solids. Add sugar and lemon juice. Stir in yeast. Siphon liquid into jugs and fit with balloons. After two months, siphon into clean jugs and cap tightly. After four months, siphon into bottles; cork.

Matures in twelve months.

RED CLOVER WINE

Red clover is found along rural roadsides, in fields and in vacant lots. The blossoms mature during mid-summer. Red clover blossoms are a popular ingredient in herb tea blends. Dry blossoms are commonly sold in natural food stores. Dried clover blossoms may be substituted for fresh, using half as much of the dried herbs as you would the newly picked.

*1 gallon red clover blossoms
(green buttons removed)*
1 gallon water
2 grapefruit
1 lime
3 lbs. sugar
½ lb. ground raisins
1 tsp. active dry yeast
1 tsp. cold strong tea

Place blossoms in crock. Boil water and pour over blossoms. Add thinly pared rinds of one grapefruit and lime, and raisins. Cover and let blossoms steep for four to five days, stirring twice daily.

Strain liquid into clean crock and add juice of two grapefruit and lime. Stir in sugar and yeast. Siphon into jugs and fit with balloons. Allow to stand until fermentation ceases, then siphon into clean jugs and cap tightly. After four months siphon into bottles, add tea, and cork.

Matures in six months.

WILD ROSE PETAL WINE

Wild roses abound throughout much of North America. The fragrant blossoms of this five-petaled flower make a delicate wine with a nice bouquet. Petals are best harvested during late morning hours after the dew has evaporated.

> *5 quarts wild rose petals*
> *2 gallons water*
> *3 lbs. sugar*
> *1 tsp. active dry yeast*
> *½ cup freshly squeezed lemon juice*

Snip white ends from gathered rose petals and place prepared petals in crock. Pour over 1½ gallons boiling water. Cover and let rest for three days, stirring occasionally. Boil two lbs. sugar in one quart of water for four minutes. Cool ten minutes, then add to petals along with yeast. Let stand for four days.

Strain through pillow case, discarding solids. Allow liquid to ferment in crock for ten days. Boil 1½ lbs. sugar in three quarts of water. Add cooled sugar water and lemon juice to rose liquid. Siphon into jugs and fit with balloons. When action ceases, siphon into clean jugs and cap tightly. Siphon into jugs after three months; cork.

Let wine age at least nine months.

WILD VIOLET WINE

Wild violets abound along streams and in damp shady forests throughout most of temperate North America. These small colorful flowers can be found blooming from May through July, depending on the elevation. Violets make a light-bodied fragrant wine.

1½ gallons wild violet blossoms
1 gallon water
2 lemons
2 oranges
3 lbs. sugar
1 tsp. active dry yeast
1½ tsp. strong tea

Boil water and pour over blossoms in crock. Add thinly pared rind of one orange and one lemon. Cover crock and allow ingredients to steep for five days, stirring occasionally.

Strain liquid into clean containers. Add sugar, juice from citrus fruit, and yeast. Allow liquid to stand in covered crock until action ceases.

Siphon liquid into jugs and add tea. Cap jugs tightly and allow to stand three months. Carefully siphon liquid into green bottles; cork.

Allow to mature eight to ten months.

Chapter IV

Wild Fruit Wine

WILD APPLE WINE

Wild apples are common roadside attractions in many rural areas of the United States and Canada. These small, tart apples make excellent wine.

1 bushel wild apples
4 lbs. sugar
1 tsp. active dry yeast
2 Tbsp. cream of tartar
½ quart brandy

Core apples and run through food grinder. Place fruit in crock and cover with clean cloth. Mash and stir daily for four days. Press out juice and return juice to cleaned crock.

Add sugar and yeast to juice, then allow to stand for three days in covered crock. Stir in cream of tartar, then siphon juice into jugs and fit with balloons. When fermentation ceases, add equal amounts of brandy to the jugs (some of the fermented liquid may need to be siphoned out in order to accommodate brandy). Cap jugs tightly. When wine has cleared, siphon into bottles. Cork.

Wild Apple Wine is now ready to serve.

WILD APPLE WINE (Dessert)

1 bushel wild apples
5 lbs. sugar
1½ grams leaf gelatin
Boiled water

Core apples and extract juice with fruit press. Measure two gallons of juice and add to kettle along with sugar. Place kettle over high heat and bring juice to boil; lower heat and simmer. Skim scum from surface frequently until no more forms. Remove kettle from heat. Add boiled water to bring liquid volume to former level. Cool. Pour into crock.

Sprinkle yeast over liquid surface in crock and allow to stand three to four days. Siphon into jugs and fit with balloons. Add equal amounts of gelatin to jugs after fermentation ceases. Cap jugs. When wine becomes clear, siphon into bottles. Cork.

Wine is ready to serve.

SPICED WILD APPLE WINE

1 bushel wild apples
2 lbs. honey
½ oz. cream of tartar
1 tsp. active dry yeast
1 oz. stick cinnamon
1 oz. whole cloves
1 whole nutmeg, cracked
¼ gallon rum

Core apples and extract juice with fruit press. Measure out two gallons of juice and add to crock along with honey and cream of tartar. Stir well before adding yeast.

Combine spices and tie in square of cheese cloth. Suspend spice bag in crock and cover crock opening. Allow to stand until all action ceases. Siphon into jugs and cap tightly. After six months, siphon into bottles. Cork.

Wine is now ready to sample.

BEACH PLUM WINE

There are over fifteen species of wild plums scattered throughout the United States and southern Canada, from Alaska and California to the eastern seaboard. Each species makes a different flavored wine.

- **4 gallons beach plums**
- **5 gallons warm water**
- **15 lbs. sugar**
- **2 oz. cream of tartar**
- **1 tsp. active dry yeast**

Pour warm water over plums in crock. Crush fruit and stir well. Allow to stand for eight hours before squeezing out juice through pillow case. Return strained juice to crock.

Add sugar and cream of tartar to juice. Stir in yeast, cover crock and allow to stand for two weeks. Skim scum, then siphon liquid into jugs. Fit with balloons. Bottle after four months.

Wine may be sampled at this time, but is better if allowed to mature for four to six months.

WILD BLACK CHERRY WINE

The wild black cherry is often called the rum cherry. During the late 1800's through the early 1900's New Englanders used the juice of these cherries to mellow the taste of raw liquors.

- **4 gallons wild black cherries (stems removed)**
- **4 lbs. sugar**

Place cherries in crock and mash thoroughly but gently, being careful not to break pits. Allow fruit to stand uncovered for 48 hours.

Press out juice, then strain through several layers of cheese cloth. Return strained juice to crock and add sugar. Cover crock with clean cloth or lid and allow fermentation to begin. After four days of action, siphon into jugs (avoiding scum) and fit with balloons. Bottle after six months.

Wine is now ready to sample

PIN CHERRY WINE

The pin cherry ranges from British Columbia to Labrador, south into the high country of Colorado, Tennessee, and North Carolina. The thick-fleshed, sour cherries make excellent wine. It is wise to bottle pin cherry wine in green bottles to protect its light red color.

6 gallons pin cherries
8 lbs. sugar
1 tsp. active dry yeast

Place cherries in crock and mash, being careful not to break pits. Allow fruit to stand for 24 hours, then squeeze and strain juice through a pillow case.

Return strained juice to crock. Add sugar and yeast. Cover crock. Stir daily until violent action ceases. Skim scum off surface of liquid, then siphon juice into jugs and fit with balloons. After five months, siphon into bottles. Cork.

Wine is now ready to sample.

CHOKECHERRY WINE

Chokecherries are found along stream banks, moist draws, and hillsides to elevations of approximately 8,000 feet throughout the United States and Canada. The fruit ripens during late summer. It is important that the fruit is harvested when completely ripe.

3 lbs. chokecherries
1 gallon water
1 tsp. active dry yeast
3½ lbs. sugar
1 tsp. cream of tartar

Stem and wash fruit. Put fruit through a food chopper or grinder. Add water and pour into a clean crock. Cover crock and let stand for three weeks, stirring often.

Carefully stir in 2½ lbs. sugar, yeast, and cream of tartar. Cover and stir twice daily. After liquid has been fermenting for two days, carefully stir in remaining sugar. Cover and let stand for seven days, then strain juice. Siphon strained juice into jugs and fit with balloons.

After action ceases, carefully siphon juice into clean jugs and cap tightly. Four months later, siphon into clean bottles; cork.

Let wine mature at least twelve months before sampling.

CHOKECHERRY WINE (Dessert)

5 gallons chokecherries
5 gallons warm water
16 lbs. sugar
2 tsp. active dry yeast

Remove stems from fruit, then put fruit through a food chopper or grinder (using coarsest blade). Place fruit in crock and pour in five gallons warm water. Add sugar and yeast. Stir daily for ten days.

Strain liquid into clean crock. Allow to rest for two days before siphoning into jugs and fitting with balloons. After three months, siphon into clean jugs and cap tightly. Two months later, siphon into bottles; cork.

Allow wine to age eight to twelve months.

PACIFIC CRABAPPLE WINE

The small, slightly bitter Pacific crabapple is not too tasty when eaten raw, but this fruit makes one of the best homemade apple wines I've ever tasted.

10 lbs. ripe Pacific crabapples, seeded
1 lb. raisins
1 gallon boiling water
½ oz. stick cinnamon
½ oz. whole cloves
4 lbs. sugar
1 tsp. active dry yeast

Put apples and raisins through food grinder. Pour over boiling water. Add cinnamon and cloves. Stir, then cover crock and allow to stand one week.

Strain through pillow case; discard pulp. Stir sugar into juice, then add yeast. Allow to stand for two days before siphoning into jugs and fitting with balloons.

After two months, siphon into clean jugs and cap tightly. Four months later, siphon into bottles; cork.

Matures in five months.

PAW PAW WINE

Wild paw paws are found growing in the Atlantic and Gulf states north to New York, Michigan, Wisconsin, and Iowa, and west Nebraska, Kansas, and Oklahoma. The paw paw trees thrive best on rich soils along river bottoms.

The outer fruit covering becomes yellow and brown when the fruit is mature (from August to November). The pulp is custard-like, cream-colored, and fragrant. When the fruit is prepared for winemaking, the paw paw is halved, the pulp scooped out, and the covering discarded. Paw paw wine has a fragrant bouquet, but many find its flavor too bland and prefer to mix it equally with a more flavorful wild wine.

4 lbs. paw paw pulp
1 gallon water
3 lbs. sugar
2 Tbsp. freshly squeezed lemon juice
2 tsp. cream of tartar
1 tsp. active dry yeast

Put pulp in crock and cover with boiling water. Cover crock and allow to stand 24 hours. Strain through pillow case, squeezing pulp as dry as possible; discard pulp. Add sugar, yeast, lemon juice, and cream of tartar. Siphon into jugs and fit with balloons.

After action has ceased, siphon into clean jugs and cap tightly. Siphon again in three months, then again in another three months. Now siphon into bottles, cork.

Allow to mature from eight months to a year.

WILD PERSIMMON WINE

The wild persimmon is found from Rhode Island to Florida, and west to Kansas and Texas. The fruit is fully ripened when it is orange-red, wrinkled and soft to the touch.

3 lbs. persimmon pulp
1 gallon water
1 lemon, thinly sliced
3 lbs. sugar
1 tsp. active dry yeast

Put pulp, lemon, and water in crock. Stir well, then cover with clean cloth or lid. Set aside and allow to stand five days.

Strain into clean crock; discard pulp. Add sugar and yeast. Cover crock and allow to stand one week. Siphon into clean jugs and fit with balloons. When action ceases, siphon into clean jugs and cap tightly. After three months, siphon into clean jugs and cap. Repeat procedure again in three months, then carefully siphon into bottles; cork.

Matures in six months.

POMEGRANATE WINE

Pomegranates have recently naturalized in parts of the southern United States. The sweet, red, juicy seeds of this fruit makes a flavorful wine. Pomegranates are prepared for winemaking by removing the seeds from the leathery skin. Be certain that all white membrane is removed for it will impart a bitter flavor to the wine.

4 lbs. pomegranate seeds
1¼ gallons water
2 tsp. grated lemon rind
4 lbs. sugar
1 tsp. active dry yeast

Place pomegranate seeds in crock. Crush seeds, then add one gallon of water and lemon rind; cover and set aside for four days.

Meanwhile, bring remaining water to boil. Add two cups of sugar. Remove from heat and cool to lukewarm. Add yeast and set aside.

Strain juice through pillow case. Discard pulp. Stir in remaining sugar. Add yeast-sugar-water mixture. Stir well, then siphon into jugs and fit with balloons.

When action ceases, siphon into clean jugs and cap tightly. After four months, siphon into bottles; cork.

Wine is ready to drink in six to eight months.

PRICKLY PEAR WINE

The red-fruited prickly pear makes a better wine than those which bear yellow or orange fruit. The fruit usually ripens between September and February. Select fruit which is plump, yet gives slightly under pressure. It is best to harvest prickly pears with a pair of heavy gloves.

> *8 lbs. prickly pear fruit*
> *3 lbs. sugar*
> *1 gallon water*
> *Juice of one lemon*
> *1 tsp. active dry yeast*

Thinly peel fruit, slice each in half and place in large kettle. Heat fruit to 160°F. Remove from heat, cool slightly, then pour into crock. Crush fruit. Cover crock and allow pulp to stand for three days, stirring twice daily. Strain and press juice into clean crock, discarding solids.

Add sugar, lemon juice, and yeast. Cover crock and allow to ferment until action ceases. Siphon liquid into jugs, filling close to the top. Be careful not to disturb the sediment in bottom of crock. After three months, siphon wine into bottles; cork.

Matures in ten to twelve months.

SLOE WINE

The cherry sized, powdery-blue colored sloe has a disagreeable flavor when eaten raw, but produces an agreeable wine. It is important to allow to fruit to ripen fully before harvesting.

3½ lbs. sloe fruit
2 cups white seedless raisins
1 gallon water
3 lbs. sugar
1 tsp. active dry yeast

Prick each sloe several times with sharp fork tines, then place in clean crock. Add raisins. Bring to boil ¾ gallon water and one pound sugar. Cool slightly, then pour over fruit in crock. Cover and allow fruit to soak for six days.

Strain liquid into clean crock. Do not squeeze fruit.

Dissolve remaining sugar in ¼ gallon of boiling water, then add to fruit. Add yeast, cover crock and allow to work for twelve days, stirring daily. Siphon liquid into jugs and fit with balloons.

When all visible action is complete, siphon liquid into clean jugs and cap tightly. Siphon several more times at three month intervals. Bottle and cork.

Allow wine to mature at least eight months.

WILD STRAWBERRY WINE

Wild strawberries are widely distributed, but because of their size, they are difficult to gather in large quantities. This tiny fruit makes an excellent wine for special occasions.

> *1 gallon wild strawberries*
> *(no stems and leaves)*
> *1 gallon water*
> *4 lbs. sugar*
> *1 tsp. active dry yeast*

Mash berries and extract juice. Bring water to boil, remove from heat, then add sugar. Pour into crock; cool before adding strawberry juice and yeast.

After violent action ceases, siphon into jugs and fit with balloons. Allow liquid to work until all action ceases. Siphon into bottles; cork.

Wine matures in six to eight weeks.

Chapter V

Wild Blends

WILD APPLE-CRANBERRY WINE

4 lbs. wild apples, cored
2 lbs. wild or commercially grown cranberries
1½ gallons boiling water
3½ lbs. sugar
1 - 6 oz. cake compressed yeast, crumbled
2 cups freshly squeezed orange juice
1 cup honey

Run apples and cranberries through food chopper, then transfer fruit to crock. Pour boiling water over fruit, cover crock and allow to stand for five days.

Meanwhile, place yeast, orange juice, and honey in jar. Secure with lid and shake well. Set aside in warm place.

Strain liquid from fruit; discard pulp. Add yeast mixture to strained liquid, then siphon into jugs and fit with balloons. After action ceases, siphon into jugs and cap tightly. After four months, siphon into bottles; cork.

Matures in eight to twelve months.

WILD APPLE-ELDERBERRY WINE

Elderberries are best when gathered after first frost.

6 lbs. wild apples
4 lbs. elderberries
1 gallon water
3 lbs. sugar
1 tsp. active dry yeast

Core apples and grind in food chopper. Remove stems from elderberries and add, along with apples, to crock.

Boil water and pour over fruit. Cool. Add sugar and stir to dissolve. Cover crock with clean cheese cloth or lid and allow to stand one week. Add yeast and allow to ferment six days.

Strain juice, discarding solids. Add yeast. Siphon into jugs and fit with balloons. Allow fermentation to continue, undisturbed, until action ceases. Carefully siphon into clean jugs, cap tightly, and allow to stand three months. Siphon into clean bottles; cork.

Allow to age two to three years.

WILD APPLE-HUCKLEBERRY WINE

Wild apples and huckleberries seldom ripen at the same time. Since this combination produces such an exciting wine, it is worth harvesting the huckleberries, then freezing them until the wild apples have ripened.

4 lbs. wild apples
3 lbs. huckleberries
1 gallon water
1 lemon
3 lbs. sugar
1 tsp. active dry yeast

Core apples and chop (a blender works well). Place apples in crock along with huckleberries. Boil water and pour over fruit. Stir well, cover and leave for six days, stirring daily.

Strain juice, squeezing pulp as dry as possible. Discard pulp. Add juice of lemon, sugar, and yeast. Cover crock and allow liquid to ferment for eight weeks. Carefully siphon liquid into jugs and cap tightly. After three months, siphon into bottles; cork.

Matures in eight to ten months.

WILD APPLE-MINT WINE

6 lbs. wild apples, cored
1 quart freshly picked mint leaves
1 gallon hot water
3 lbs. sugar

Put apples and mint leaves through food chopper, then place in crock, along with hot water. Cover crock with clean cloth or lid and allow to stand for five days.

Add sugar and stir to dissolve. Cover crock and allow to stand one week. Strain liquid into clean crock, discarding solids. Siphon liquid into jugs and fit with balloons. After eight weeks, remove balloons and siphon liquid into clean jugs. Cap tightly. Four months later carefully siphon wine into bottles; cork.

Matures in six months.

WILD APPLE AND PLUM WINE

4 lbs. wild apples, cored
4 lbs. wild plums, pitted
1½ gallons water
5 lbs. sugar
1 tsp. active dry yeast

Put apples and plums through food chopper, then transfer fruit to crock. Add water and 2½ lbs. sugar. Cover crock and allow to stand for five days.

Strain through pillow case. Discard solids. Add remaining sugar to liquid and stir well to dissolve. Allow crock to stand covered for five days. If fermentation has failed to begin, remove one pint of liquid from crock and add yeast. Stir well. Set yeast mixture in warm place until action starts. Stir yeast mixture into liquid in crock.

Siphon liquid into jugs and fit with balloons. When action ceases, siphon into clean jugs and cap tightly. Allow to stand three months before siphoning into bottles and corking.

Matures in ten to twelve months.

WILD APPLE-ROSE HIP WINE

6 lbs. wild apples
3 lbs. wild rose hips
1 orange, unpeeled
1 gallon boiling water
3 lbs. sugar
1 tsp. cream of tartar
1 tsp. active dry yeast

Core apples. Put apples, rose hips, and orange through food chopper. Place chopped fruit in crock and pour boiling water over. Stir and cover. Allow to stand three days, stirring occasionally.

Strain pulp into clean crock, discarding pulp. Add sugar and cream of tartar. Stir in yeast. Siphon into jugs and fit with balloons. Allow to stand until action ceases, then siphon into clean jugs and cap tightly. After three months, siphon into bottles; cork. Matures in six months.

BLACKBERRY-WILD APPLE WINE

    2 gallons blackberries
    2 lbs. wild apples, cored and grated
    2 gallons boiling water
    3½ lbs. sugar
    1 tsp. active dry yeast

    Place berries and grated apples in crock. Crush fruit, then add water. Cover crock and allow to stand four days, stirring daily.
    Strain liquid through pillow case, discarding solids. Add sugar and stir well. Add yeast, cover crock and allow to stand for five days, stirring daily.
    Siphon into jugs and fit with balloons. When action ceases, remove balloons and tightly cap bottles. After three months, siphon into bottles and cork.
    Matures in five months.

BLACKBERRY-ELDERBERRY WINE

    8 lbs. blackberries
    4 lbs. elderberries (stems removed)
    2 gallons warm water
    5 lbs. sugar
    1 tsp. active dry yeast

    Place berries in crock and crush well. Cover with warm water. Cover and allow to stand for 48 hours, stirring occasionally.
    Strain juice into clean crock, discarding pulp. Add sugar and yeast, then cover and allow to stand three days, stirring frequently.
    Siphon into jugs and fit with balloons. After fermentation ceases, remove balloons and tightly cap jugs. After four months, siphon into bottles, avoiding sediment on bottom, and cork.
    Matures in eight months (improves with age).

BLACKBERRY-SALAL WINE

Blackberries and salal both ripen in late August and are usually found along the coastal areas of the Pacific Northwest, growing within a short distance of one another.

Novice winemakers have good results with this blend, ending with a full-bodied, fragrant wine.

2 gallons blackberries
1 gallon salal berries, stems removed
1 gallon hot water
3½ lbs. sugar

Place berries in crock and mash well. Add water, stir, and cover. Allow to stand for four days, stirring daily. Add 1½ lbs. sugar; cover and allow to stand six days.

Strain juice through pillow case. Discard solids. Cover strained liquid and allow to stand for four days. Siphon into jugs and fit with balloons. When action ceases, siphon into clean jugs and cap tightly. Siphon again in three months. After two months, carefully siphon into bottles; cork.

Matures in four to six months.

BLACKBERRY-SUMACH WINE

4 lbs. blackberries
2 lbs. sumach berries
1 gallon boiling water
3½ lbs. sugar

Place berries in crock and cover with boiling water. Mash berries, cover crock and allow to stand one week, stirring occasionally.

Strain into clean crock through pillow case, discarding pulp. Remove from crock two quarts juice and place in saucepan over medium heat. Add sugar to juice in saucepan and heat until sugar is dissolved. Remove from heat and cool to lukewarm. Stir into juice in crock, cover crock and allow to stand one week.

Siphon into jugs and fit with balloons. After action ceases, siphon into clean jugs and cap tightly. Four months later, siphon into clean jugs and cap. Siphon into bottles at the end of three months. Cork.

Matures in two to four months.

CAMOMILE-RED CLOVER WINE

*2 qts. camomile blossoms
(no green parts or stems)
2 qts. red clover blossoms
(no green parts or stems)
1 gallon boiling water
2 oranges, finely chopped
(rind included)
3 lbs. sugar
1 tsp. active dry yeast*

    Place blossoms in crock and pour in boiling water. Add oranges and stir well. Cover crock with clean cloth or lid and allow to stand 48 hours, stirring occasionally.
    Strain liquid into clean crock and discard solids. Add sugar and yeast, cover crock and allow to stand for three days. Stirring daily.
    Siphon fermenting liquid into jugs and fit with balloons. When fermentation ceases, remove balloons and cap jugs tightly. After three months, siphon into clean jugs and cap. Three months later, siphon into bottles; cork.
    Matures in ten to twelve months (gets better with age).

ELDERFLOWER-MINT WINE

3 qts. elderflower petals
1 qt. wild mint leaves, lightly packed
1 gallon boiling water
2½ lbs. sugar
1 lb. honey
3 cups freshly squeezed orange juice
1 tsp. active dry yeast

Put petals and leaves in crock and cover with one gallon boiling water. Cover crock and allow to stand for 48 hours, stirring occasionally.

Meanwhile, combine honey, orange juice and yeast in jar. Shake well and set aside in warm place.

Strain blossom liquid through pillow case, discarding solids. Add sugar and stir well to dissolve. Stir in yeast mixture. Siphon into jugs and fit with balloons. When action ceases, siphon liquid into clean jugs and cap tightly. Siphon again in three months. After four months, siphon into bottles; cork.

Matures in two to three years.

LEMON GRASS-PEPPERMINT WINE

    3 qts. lemon grass (4 oz. dried)
    1½ qts. peppermint leaves (2½ oz. dried)
    1½ gallons boiling water
    2 lbs. sugar
    2 lbs. honey
    1 tsp. active dry yeast
    2 cups freshly squeezed orange juice

  Place lemon grass and peppermint leaves in crock. Cover with 1½ gallons boiling water. Cover crock and allow to stand for 24 hours.
  Meanwhile, combine honey, yeast, and orange juice. Set aside.
  Strain herb liquid through pillow case, discarding solids. Add sugar and honey-yeast mixture to strained liquid. Cover crock and allow to stand for 24 hours.
  Siphon into jugs and fit with balloons. After action ceases, siphon into clean jugs and cap tightly. Four months later, siphon into bottles; cork.
  Matures in one to one and one half years.

WILD MINT-CAMOMILE WINE

    3 quarts wild mint leaves
    1½ quarts comomile blossoms
    1 gallon boiling water
    3½ lbs. sugar
    1 tsp. active dry yeast
    1 cup freshly squeezed orange juice

  Place mint and camomile in crock and cover with one gallon boiling water. Cover crock and allow to steep 24 hours.
  Meanwhile, combine 2 cups sugar with yeast and orange juice in jar. Shake well, then set aside in warm place.
  Strain herb liquid, discarding solids. Stir remaining sugar into strained liquid, then add yeast mixture. Cover crock and allow to stand for 24 hours.
  Siphon liquid into clean jugs and fit with balloons. When action ceases, siphon into clean jugs and cap tightly. After three months, siphon into bottles; cork. Matures in ten to twelve months.

WILD MINT-ELDERBERRY WINE

½ gallon mint leaves
½ gallon elderberries (stems removed)
1½ gallons boiling water
2 lbs. honey
1½ lbs. sugar
1 tsp. active dry yeast

Place mint and berries in crock. Mash well. Cover with 1½ gallons boiling water. Cover crock and allow to stand for three days, stirring daily.

Siphon into jugs and fit with balloons. After action ceases, remove balloons and cap tightly. Four months later, siphon into clean jugs, cap and allow to stand three months. Siphon into bottles; cork. Matures in one to two years (gets better with age).

RED CLOVER-GOLDEN ROD WINE

1 gallon red clover blossoms
  (no stems or green parts)
½ gallon golden rod blossoms
  (no stems or green parts)
1 gallon boiling water
3 lbs. sugar
½ gallon freshly squeezed orange juice
1 tsp. active dry yeast

Place clover and golden rod in crock and cover with one gallon boiling water. Add sugar and stir to dissolve. Cover crock and allow to stand for three to four days, stirring daily.

Strain liquid through pillow case, discarding solids. Remove one pint strained liquid to jar, then stir in orange juice and yeast. Set aside in warm place. After two days, stir into strained liquid.

Siphon liquid into jugs and fit with balloons. After fermentation ceases, siphon into clean jugs and cap tightly. After three months, siphon again and allow to stand for three months longer. Siphon into bottles; cork.

Matures in ten months.

ROSE HIP-BLACKBERRY WINE

    4 lbs. rose hips
    3 lbs. blackberries
    1 gallon boiling water
    2½ lbs. sugar
    1 lemon, thinly sliced
    1 tsp. active dry yeast

    Put rose hips and blackberries through food chopper. Place fruit in crock along with sugar and boiling water. Stir well, cool, then add lemon and yeast. Cover crock and allow to ferment for nine days.
    Strain liquid through pillow case, discarding pulp. Carefully siphon strained liquid into jugs and fit with balloons. After three months, siphon into clean jugs and cap tightly. After three months, siphon into bottles; cork.
    Allow wine to mature at least eight months.

ROSE HIP-MINT WINE

    Rose hips and mint blend well together to make an exciting dessert wine.

    4 lbs. rose hips
    3 cups freshly picked mint leaves
    3½-lbs. sugar
    1 gallon water
    1 lemon, thinly sliced
    1 tsp. active dry yeast
    1 Tbsp. strong tea

    Place rose hips and mint in crock; cover with one gallon boiling water. Add sliced lemon. Cover crock and allow to stand for 48 hours. Crush rose hips and mint, then strain liquid into clean crock, discarding solids.
    Add sugar to strained liquid. Add yeast and stir well. Cover crock and allow to stand for 24 hours. Siphon fermenting liquid into jugs and fit with balloons. After action ceases, siphon into clean jugs and add tea. Three months later, siphon into bottles. Cork.
    Wine is ready to sample in eight months.

ROSE HIP-SALAL WINE

4 lbs. rose hips
2½ lbs. salal berries (stems removed)
1½ gallons boiling water
2 oranges, thinly sliced
4 lbs. sugar
1 tsp. active dry yeast

Run rose hips and berries through food grinder. Place ground fruit in crock and cover with 1½ gallons boiling water. Add oranges. Cover crock and allow to stand for three days, stirring daily.

Strain liquid, discarding solids. Add sugar and yeast, then cover crock and allow to stand for four days. Stirring daily.

Siphon into jugs and fit with balloons. After action ceases, siphon into clean jugs and cap tightly. Allow to stand four months before siphoning into bottles and corking.

Matures in eight months.

SALAL-WILD APPLE WINE

Salal ripens just as the wild roadside apples develop into hard, tart fruit. The tartness of the apples compliment the sweet bland berries of the salal. Wine made from this combination is excellent!

3 lbs. salal berries (no stems)
3 lbs. wild apples
2½ gallons water
3 lbs. sugar
1 tsp. active dry yeast

Slice apples, removing seeds, and place them in large kettle along with the salal berries. Pour water over fruit, place on stove, then bring to boil over medium heat. Remove from heat and cool a few minutes before pouring into clean crock.

When mixture has cooled, mash fruit. Cover and allow fruit to steep for four days, stirring frequently. Strain juice through pillow case, squeezing pulp as dry as possible. Discard solids. Add sugar and yeast, then siphon into jugs. Fit jugs with balloons and allow to stand undisturbed until action ceases.

Siphon into clean jugs and cap tightly. After three months, siphon into bottles; cork.

Matures in eight months (improves with age).

SALAL-ELDERBERRY WINE

5 lbs. salal berries (stems removed)
3 lbs. elderberries
2 gallons boiling water
5 lbs. sugar
1 tsp. active dry yeast

Mash berries in crock, then add boiling water. Cover crock and allow to stand for 48 hours, stirring occasionally.

Strain liquid through pillow case, discarding solids. Add sugar and yeast to strained liquid, cover crock and allow to stand 24 hours.

Siphon into jugs and fit with balloons. Allow to stand until action ceases. Siphon into clean jugs and cap tightly. After four months, siphon into bottles; cork.

Matures in two to three years.

SALAL-PACIFIC CRAB APPLE WINE

Both salal and the Pacific crab apple are abundant west of the Cascade Mountains and along the Northwestern Pacific Coast. They mature during late August through early September. Their combined flavors make an agreeable table wine.

5 lbs. salal berries
3 lbs. Pacific crab apples, seeded
2 gallons boiling water
2 Tbsp. cream of tartar
5 lbs. sugar
1 tsp. active dry yeast

Run berries and apples through food grinder. Place ground fruit in crock and cover with two gallons boiling water. Cover crock and let stand three days, stirring daily.

Strain through pillow case, discarding solids. Stir in cream of tartar, sugar and yeast. Cover crock and allow to stand 24 hours, stirring occasionally.

Siphon into jugs and fit with balloons. When action ceases, remove balloons and cap jugs tightly. After three months, siphon into clean jugs; cap. Three months later, siphon into bottle and cork.

Matures in eight to ten months.

SUMACH-ROSE HIP WINE

    4 lbs. sumach berries
    3 lbs. rose hips
    1½ gallons boiling water
    2 lbs. honey
    2 lbs. sugar
    2 pints freshly squeezed orange juice
    1 tsp. active dry yeast

  Run berries and rose hips through food chopper, then add to crock along with boiling water. Cover crock and allow to stand 48 hours, stirring occasionally.
  Meanwhile, combine one cup honey with orange juice and yeast. Mix well, cover and put in warm place.
  Strain liquid through pillow case, discarding solids. Add remaining honey and sugar. Stir well. Add yeast mixture, and stir again.
  Siphon into jugs and fit with balloons. When action ceases, siphon into clean jugs and cap tightly. After three months, siphon into clean bottles; cork.
  Matures in eight to ten months.

Chapter VI

Miscellaneous Wild Wine

BIRCH SAP WINE

Birsh sap is tapped during March. Locate a birch tree with a trunk seven inches in diameter. Drill a ½" in diameter hole one foot from the base of the tree. Insert one end of a section of rubber hose or surgical tubing into the hole and put the opposite end of the hose or tubing into a glass jug. It will take a few days to gather a sufficient supply of sap. The hole should be plugged with a cork after sap has been gathered.

5 pints birch sap
2½ lbs. sugar
2 lemons
2 cups raisins
½ gallon water
1 cup freshly squeezed orange juice
1 tsp. active dry yeast

Combine birch sap and sugar in large kettle. Put lemons and raisins through food chopper. Add to kettle. Bring kettle contents to boil, reduce heat and simmer ten minutes.

Pour into crock and add water. Stir yeast into orange juice, then stir juice into sap mixture. Cover crock with clean cloth or lid and allow to ferment for four days, stirring daily.

Strain through pillow case, discarding solids. Siphon strained liquid into jugs and fit with balloons. After four months, carefully siphon into bottles; cork.

Wine is now ready to sample, but improves with age.

WILD CHERRY BARK WINE

Wild cherry bark may be gathered directly from the tree or purchased in a natural food store. Do not strip bark from a live tree as this may destroy the plant.

4 oz. wild cherry bark
1 gallon water
1 lb. red wheat
1 lb. ground raisins
3 lemons, thinly sliced
3½ lbs. sugar
1 tsp. active dry yeast

Place bark and wheat in crock; cover with one gallon boiling water. Cover crock and allow to steep for five days, stirring frequently. Drain off liquid, discarding solids.

Add raisins and lemons to drained liquid. Stir in sugar, then sprinkle yeast over surface. Allow to stand, covered, three weeks, stirring daily.

After three weeks, strain liquid, discarding solids, and siphon into jugs. Fit jugs with balloons. When action ceases, siphon into clean jugs and cap tightly. Four months later, siphon into bottles; cork.

Allow wine to age at least eight months.

COMFREY WINE

Comfrey, a garden herb once mainly grown for its medicinal properties, has naturalized throughout the moderate temperature zones of North America. This unusual wine is relished by many who try it.

25 comfrey roots
5 gallons water
15 lbs. sugar
2 lemons
2 tsp. active dry yeast

Wash and peel roots. Cut into ½" pieces. Place in kettle, along with water, and bring to boil. Reduce heat and simmer until roots are tender, skimming frequently. Strain liquid through pillow case into clean crock. Add sugar; cool and add yeast.

Cover crock with cloth or lid and allow to stand seven days, stirring daily. Siphon into jugs and fit with balloons. After four months, siphon into clean jugs and cap tightly. Allow to clarify another three months, then siphon into bottles; cork.

Wine matures in eight months.

WILD FENNEL WINE

Wild fennel has feathery-like foliage and a mild licorice aroma. The roots make an unusual wine prized by natural food fanciers.

> ½ lb. freshly gathered wild fennel root
>   (scrubbed and chopped)
> 1 gallon water
> 3 lbs. honey
> 1 to 1½ gallons well boiled water

Place fennel roots, one gallon water, and honey in large kettle. Bring to boil over high heat. Reduce heat and boil gently for 45 minutes. Strain liquid into clean kettle, adding enough boiled water to make up for that which was lost through evaporation.

Bring liquid to boil and simmer for two more hours, skimming frequently. At the end of two hours, add enough boiled water to make up for water lost through evaporation.

Cool liquid to lukewarm before siphoning into jugs. Fit with balloons and allow to stand ten to twelve months. Siphon into bottles; cork.

Wine is now ready to drink.

WILD MINT WINE

There are numerous varieties of wild mint native to North America. Wild mint is most often found growing along stream banks and in meadows. This wine makes a refreshing beverage and is a perfect companion for light desserts.

1 gallon freshly picked mint leaves
5 gallons cold water
15 lbs. sugar
2 tsp. active dry yeast

Lightly pack mint leaves in crock. Pour over cold water, sugar, and yeast. Cover crock and set in warm place (68° to 72°) for ten to twelve days, stirring daily.

Strain liquid through pillow case, then siphon strained liquid into jugs. Fit with balloons. Allow to ferment until action ceases, then siphon into jugs and cap tightly. After three months, siphon into bottles; cork.

Mint wine will be ready to drink in four to six months.

NETTLE WINE

Stinging nettles, one of the most nutritious green plants, make an agreeable table wine. The young nettles are gathered in the spring when they have reached between three to six inches in heighth. A sufficient supply of nettles can be quickly harvested if gloves are worn to avoid stings.

3 gallons stinging nettles
4 gallons water
10 lbs. sugar
1 tsp. active dry yeast

Place nettles in crock. Boil four gallons water and pour over nettles. Add sugar; cool, then add yeast. Cover crock and allow to stand five days, stirring occasionally.

Siphon liquid into jugs and fit with balloons. Allow to rest for ten weeks before siphoning into clean jugs and capping tightly. After four months, siphon into bottles; cork.

Wine matures in six months.

SARSAPARILLA WINE

Beverages made from sarsaparilla were a part of early Americana. Wine produced from sarsaparilla will not only bring nostalgic memories but smiles of delight, as well.

> 1 lb. *sarsaparilla leaves and stems*
> 1 *gallon water*
> ¼ lb. *chopped raisins*
> 2 lbs. *sugar*
> 1 *lemon, thinly sliced*
> 1 tsp. *active dry yeast*

Place sarasparilla in crock and pour water over. Mash well before adding raisins, sugar, lemons, and yeast. Allow to work in open crock for five to six days.

Strain liquid through pillow case, discarding solids. Siphon into jugs and fit with balloons. After fermentation ceases, carefully siphon into clean jugs and cap tightly. Allow to clarify for three months before carefully siphoning into bottles. Cork.

Wine will be ready to sample in six months.

SASSAFRAS WINE

Sassafras is most commonly found in the Northeastern states. The first colonists of Massachusetts shipped large quantities of the root and bark to Europe where its main uses were medicinal and flavoring.

Wine, along with tea and root beer, is made from the root bark of the sassafras tree. This bark is sold in natural food stores and may be substituted for freshly gathered bark in winemaking.

3 oz. dried sassafras root bark
1 gallon water
1 lb. barley
1 lb. raisins
3 lemons
3 lbs. sugar
1 tsp. active dry yeast

Place bark and barley in crock; boil water and pour over. Cover crock and allow to steep for five days, stirring frequently. Drain off liquid, discarding solids.

In sterilized food chopper, chop together lemons and raisins. Stir in sugar and yeast, then add to drained liquid, stirring gently. Allow to stand covered for three weeks.

Strain liquid through pillow case, discarding solids. Siphon strained liquid into jugs and fit with balloons. When fermentation has ceased, carefully siphon into clean jugs and cap tightly. Siphon again in three months. After four months, carefully siphon into bottles; cork.

Matures in eight to ten months.

INDEX

Wild Berry Wine

Blackberry Wine 9
Blackberry Wine (dessert) 10
Blackcap Wine 10
Blueberry Wine 11
Crowberry Wine 12
Wild Currant Wine 13
Wild Currant Wine (dessert) 14
Dewberry Wine 14
Elderberry Wine 15
Elderberry Wine (dessert) 16
Elderberry Wine, Spiced 16
European Red Hawthorne Wine 17
Wild Gooseberry Wine 18
Wild Grape Wine 19
Wild Grape Wine (sparkling) 20
Wild Grape Wine (dessert) 20
Wild Grape Wine, Spiced 21
Highbush Cranberry Wine 22
Huckleberry Wine 23
Loganberry Wine 24
Loganberry Wine, Spiced 24
Mountain Ash Wine 25
Mountain Cranberry Wine 26
Oregon Grape Wine 27
Red Huckleberry Wine 28
Red Mulberry Wine 28
Wild Red Raspberry Wine 29
Wild Rose Hip Wine 30
Wild Rose Hip Wine, Spiced 31
Salal Wine 32
Salal Wine, Spiced 33
Salmonberry Wine 34

Sea Grape Wine 35
Serviceberry Wine 36
Sumach Wine 37
Thimbleberry Wine............................... 38

Wild Flower Wine

Roadside Apple Blossom Wine..................... 39
Camomile Wine 40
Cowslip Wine................................... 41
Wild Daisy Wine................................ 42
Dandelion Wine 43
Dandelion Wine (dessert) 43
Dogwood Blossom Wine 44
Elderflower Wine 45
Elderflower Wine (dessert) 46
Golden Rod Wine 47
Hibiscus Flower Wine 48
Honeysuckle Wine.............................. 49
Lavender Blossom Wine 50
Milkweed Blossom Wine 51
Pomegranate Blossom Wine...................... 52
Red Clover Wine 53
Wild Rose Petal Wine............................ 54
Wild Violet Wine 55

Wild Fruit Wine

Wild Apple Wine 57
Wild Apple Wine (dessert) 58
Wild Apple Wine, Spiced 58
Beach Plum Wine 59
Wild Black Cherry Wine 59
Pin Cherry Wine 60
Chokecherry Wine 61
Chokecherry Wine (dessert) 62
Pacific Crab Apple Wine......................... 62
Paw Paw Wine 63
Wild Persimmon Wine 64
Pomegranate Wine 65
Prickly Pear Wine............................... 66
Sloe Wine 67
Wild Strawberry Wine 68

Wild Blends

Wild Apple-Cranberry Wine 69
Wild Apple-Elderberry Wine 70
Wild Apple-Huckleberry Wine 71
Wild Apple-Mint Wine 71
Wild Apple and Plum Wine 72
Wild Apple-Rose Hip Wine 72
Blackberry-Wild Apple Wine 73
Blackberry-Elderberry Wine 73
Blackberry-Salal Wine 74
Blackberry-Sumach Wine 74
Camomile-Red Clover Wine 75
Elderflower-Mint Wine 76
Lemon Grass-Peppermint Wine 77
Wild Mint-Camomile Wine 77
Wild Mint-Elderberry Wine 78
Red Clover-Golden Rod Wine 78
Rose Hip-Blackberry Wine 79
Rose Hip-Mint Wine 79
Rose Hip-Salal Wine 80
Salal-Wild Apple Wine 81
Salal-Elderberry Wine 82
Salal-Pacific Crab Apple Wine 82
Sumach-Rose Hip Wine 83

Misc. Wild Wine

Birch Sap Wine 85
Wild Cherry Bark Wine 86
Comfrey Wine 87
Wild Fennel Wine 88
Wild Mint Wine 89
Nettle Wine 90
Sarsaparilla Wine 91
Sassafras Wine 92